Public Speaking Anxiety
How to Face the Fear

L. Todd Thomas, Ph.D.

Harcourt Brace College Publishers

Fort Worth   Philadelphia   San Diego   New York   Orlando   Austin   San Antonio
Toronto   Montreal   London   Sydney   Tokyo

Publisher	Christopher P. Klein
Senior Acquisitions Editor	Carol Wada
Editorial Assistant	Scott Stephens
Project Editor	Catherine Townsend
Production Manager	Jane Tyndall Ponceti
Art Director	David A. Day

Copyright © 1997 by Harcourt Brace & Company

All rights reserved. No part of this publication may be reproduced or transmitted in any form or by any means, electronic or mechanical, including photocopy, recording, or any information storage and retrieval system, without permission in writing from the publisher.

Requests for permission to make copies of any part of the work should be mailed to: Permissions Department, Harcourt Brace & Company, 6277 Sea Harbor Drive, Orlando, FL 32887-6777.

Harcourt Brace College Publishers may provide complimentary instructional aids and supplements or supplement packages to those adopters qualified under our adoption policy. Please contact your sales representative for more information. If as an adopter or potential user you receive supplements you do not need, please return them to your sales representative or send them to: Attn: Returns Department, Troy Warehouse, 465 South Lincoln Drive, Troy, MO 63379.

Address for Editorial Correspondence: Harcourt Brace College Publishers, 301 Commerce Street, Suite 3700, Fort Worth, TX 76102.

Address for Orders: Harcourt Brace & Company, 6277 Sea Harbor Drive, Orlando, FL 32887. 1-800-782-4479, or 1-800-433-0001 (in Florida)

ISBN: 0-03-018243-3
Printed in the United States of America

7 8 9 0 1 2 3 4 5 066 10 9 8 7 6 5 4 3

Contents

Introduction 1

Chapter One
The Public Speaking Experience 3

Chapter Two
Mind and Body 9

Chapter Three
What We Know and What We *Think* We Know 15

Chapter Four
Nervous Excitement versus Nervous Anxiety 21

Chapter Five
Presenting the Speech 33

Chapter Six
The Final Word 41

Introduction

My greatest weakness is the fear to speak in front of people. In one case, I made an excuse that I had a dentist appointment just so I wouldn't have to speak in front of the people where I work. Another thing that bothers me about speaking in front of people is that I'm afraid that I will make a fool out of myself or that I look stupid or sound stupid. What I want is to be able to walk up in front of a crowd and feel comfortable enough that my voice doesn't crack and I can give a smooth presentation without being scared to death.

—JIM, 35

I have never been able to get up in front of people without being scared to death. I had a speech class in high school and it was a very bad experience. I was extremely nervous with every speech I gave. I would tremble and shake; I even felt faint and very hot. My voice tends to be soft when I talk and I also talk very fast. As a speaker right now, I think I am horrible.

—MELISSA, 23

Do these stories sound familiar to you? Would *you* rather go to the dentist than give a public speech? If so, you might be one of the tens of thousands of people who experience public speaking anxiety. Study after study has indicated that one of the most common fears in today's society is the fear of standing in front of a group of people to give a presentation. Research indicates that more than 85 percent of the population experience anxiety when faced with giving a public speech, while as many as 20 percent identify this anxiety as severe. For some, a slight nervousness makes the experience a bit uncomfortable. For others, even the *idea* of speaking in public is terrifying.

It is likely that you experience some sort of nervousness when facing a public presentation. It might be that you are one of those people who find that this nervousness adds to the excitement of the situation. On the other hand, you may feel that your anxiety about giving a public speech is totally overwhelming. What is more likely is that your anxiety about public speaking interferes with your ability to enjoy the experience of giving a speech and that you would like to find a way to help make the speech experience more pleasant and effective.

This book is designed to help you examine your anxiety about public speaking and develop some strategies for coping with this anxiety. We are first going to discuss the problems associated with public speaking anxiety. We will then cover some of the common symptoms and responses you may have experienced as a result of your speech anxiety, followed by some common misconceptions about public speaking in general. Finally, we will discuss some methods you can use to make your public speaking experiences more enjoyable and more successful.

Chapter One
The Public Speaking Experience

One of the key elements in understanding and dealing with anxiety about public speaking is understanding the process we go through when faced with the possibility of giving a presentation. For some, this process leads to an enjoyable and successful experience, while for others the process is painful and laborious. Whether enjoyable or not, the public speaking *experience* usually starts long before the public speaking *event*.

Most of us do not even think about public speaking until we find ourselves faced with the *possibility* that we are going to give a speech. The word "possibility" is emphasized because we do not necessarily have to face the reality of public speaking to get anxious. If we even think there is any *chance* we may have to give a speech, the feelings of dread can begin.

For many people, the thought of giving a speech can bring physical discomfort. Katie describes her experience:

I start getting nervous weeks before [the speech]. The same thing always happens. My stomach knots up and hurts like I have an ulcer or something. I go through nights where I can't get to sleep. Then there will be days when I can't stay awake. I remember when I first interviewed for this job and the personnel manager asked me if I had ever given a speech. I told him that I had, but inside I could feel my stomach knotting up again. Stupid, huh? He didn't ask me to give a speech, he just asked me if I ever had!

Even before the awareness begins, we already have the foundation for our public speaking experience: our assumptions about the nature of public speaking in general. We will discuss these assumptions in detail later, but for now we can divide them into two distinct schools of thought. The first is the **Piece-of-Cake** philosophy. The speaker who has these assumptions about public speaking sees no challenge in giving a presentation to a group of people. If there is a lot riding on the outcome of the speech, this speaker may be slightly nervous, but not too much. This speaker feels that making a speech is not difficult at all. All you have to do is undertake a little bit of research, make a few notes, pick out some nice clothing, and show up to give the speech. Nothing to it.

The second school of thought is the **Eating Glass** philosophy. For this speaker, there is absolutely, positively, no way on earth that the speech can be a success. This speaker feels that the only people who give good speeches are *other* people. This speaker feels that if he or she had wanted to be an actor, then he or she would have gone to acting school. The idea of performing in front of a group, strangers or friends, is horrifying. This speaker often is not the least bit worried about the research part of the project. However, it does not matter how exciting or compelling the material turns out to be, this speaker is convinced that a bored audience will be the outcome.

Interestingly enough, both these types of speakers, Cake and Glass, are erroneous in their assumptions. At least they are wrong in the degree to which they feel strongly about the experience of public speaking. Cake is probably going to discover that the public speaking event requires a lot more thought and a lot more planning and preparation than she thinks at this point. Glass, on the other hand, would be relieved to discover that the actual public speaking event is rarely as bad as he thinks it is going to be. Luckily, most people have assumptions that fall somewhere in between Cake and Glass.

Either way, these assumptions will immediately come forward to help us form the assessment of our personal ability when we discover that we may be chosen (or may have the opportunity) to give a public speech. You can see now how this can be a problem, especially if you tend to have the assumptions that our speaker Glass had earlier. If we assume that the public speaking event is a performance, then we immediately begin putting a lot of pressure on ourselves to "perform." We begin to think of ourselves more as actors, and we focus on the fact that there will be many pairs of eyes staring straight at us as we stand in front of them, trying our best to be great orators. As we assess our abilities, we imagine the lights and the focus of attention. We think about the "What would happen if I . . ." scenarios and start imagining possible problems that could occur during our speech. By doing this, if we are like Glass, we will find that our self-assessment comes quite short of what we think a speaker's abilities should be to give a successful public presentation. Again, we will discuss this assessment more thoroughly later, but let's move now through the rest of the public speaking experience.

Once we have made our initial self-assessment based on our assumptions about public speaking and our evaluation of our own skills, we then decide if

Same event, different expectations

we are truly capable of giving a good public speech. As the diagram near the end of this chapter shows, the answer to this question guides the outcome of our experience. If we decide that we are indeed capable of giving a successful presentation, then the nervousness we feel next will probably be best categorized as **excitement.** If we decide that we do not have the ability to give a good speech, then our nervousness becomes **anxiety.**

It's important to remember that our self-assessment is rarely, if ever, totally accurate. In fact, considering that we have not even begun putting together the speech yet, our self-assessment is based on the *assumptions* we have about our ability to do a speech. And our understanding of our ability to do the speech is based on the *assumptions* we have about public speaking. So you can see that we may already be far removed from the reality of the situation through all of these assumptions.

Now, if our assumptions lead us to the possible belief that we can indeed give a public speech successfully, then the resulting excitement will probably lead us to active, motivated preparation of our speech. If we had a public speaking class earlier in life, we might try to find the old textbook or materials we used. We might go to the bookstore and see what books are available on the subject of writing a speech. The excitement that is involved in public speaking can lead us to interesting time spent in the library reading up on the topic, or perhaps to a few hours talking with experts or other relevant individuals on the subject.

On the other hand, if we doubt our ability to do well, then the anxiety related to public speaking can lead us to near lethargy. We find that we are unable to get started on the speech because we greatly dread the time when we are going to step in front of the audience.

Avoidance becomes a key coping mechanism for many people at this point in time. Avoiding public speaking might mean avoiding the situation altogether, putting themselves in a position never to have to consider giving a presentation. For those like Monica, this avoidance can take extreme proportions with extreme consequences:

> *I worked for a health agency and had tried for a long time to get the opportunity to make a sales presentation to a local bank. After several weeks of making phone contact, I finally was able to schedule the presentation. Although I've never been comfortable speaking to a group of people, I thought that this would be different since I had so much to gain from the experience. However, as the day grew closer I became more and more nervous. On the day of the presentation, I went into the conference room to set up my overhead and flip chart equipment. As everybody came into the room, the feeling of panic became almost overwhelming. Just before the chairman was going to introduce me, I told him I needed to step to the ladies' room for a minute. I walked out of the conference room, out of the bank, got into my car and went home. I never went back to the bank and, in fact, never went back to that health agency.*

For others, eventually giving a speech is inevitable. For these people, avoidance takes on a different appearance. These people put off preparing for the speech. **Procrastination** develops from our fear of doing a poor job. This procrastination can begin before we even start formulating our speech, leaving ourselves with little time to actually get our thoughts together. In addition, since the thing most people dread most is the *performance* of the speech, procrastination can lead to a host of excuses that keeps us from practicing our speech ahead of time. Kerry's reaction is typical:

> *When I find out I have to give a presentation, I initially want for myself to do well. But in the back of my mind, I contradict that*

and know I will do poorly. I think to myself, "I can't speak in front of these people. These people will think I am boring. They won't like what I am speaking about, etc." As a result, I usually can't bring myself to even start working on the speech until there is finally no choice.

This **passive preparation** and **procrastination** will often lead us to the very thing we fear the most—an unsuccessful public speaking event. Actually, for most people who experience public speaking anxiety, even a successful public speaking event can feel like an unsuccessful one. On the day or night of the event, we discover that not only are we fearful of making a fool of ourselves, we are not as prepared as we should be and have thus increased the odds that our experience will be an awkward one. Then, regardless of whether or not the audience was pleased with the speech, we will give ourselves a post-speech **negative assessment.** This negative assessment is then filed in our brains for future public speaking opportunities.

If, on the other hand, we have convinced ourselves that we are capable of giving a good speech, then we are more likely to have spent time preparing our speech, practicing our presentation, and focusing on making our audience understand our information or point of view. As a result, we have increased the odds that we will have a positive public speaking experience and, as a result, we give ourselves a post-speech **positive assessment.** This positive assessment goes in the same "file drawer" in our brains as the negative assessment mentioned earlier, except that now the positive assessment will serve to encourage us the next time we face a public speaking event.

The good news here is that these two ways of approaching a public speech are actually not so far removed from one another. Imagine that the preceding diagram represents two hallways leading from the assessment of your personal ability to the final outcome assessment after the speech. Imagine there are several doors that connect the hallways as well. For example, you can learn to turn your anxiety into excitement and, by so doing, go through the door into the hallway leading to a successful public speaking event. You can also learn how to change your passive preparation and procrastination into a more active and effective preparation for your speech. By doing this, you will allow yourself to open the door into the hallway leading to success, positive self-assessment, and as a result, more success in the future.

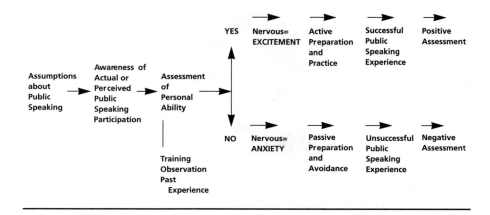

Of course, all of this is easy to say. The real trick is to be able to put your mind and body into action. You have already taken the first step by purchasing this book. Perhaps you have a speech coming up soon and want to work on the experience now. Or maybe you've just finished a speech and want a better experience next time. Regardless of when your last speech was, or when your next one is going to be, the next step is to identify what your mind and body actually do at the **awareness stage** of the public speaking experience. As you will see in the next chapter, the mind and body do a lot!

Chapter Two
Mind and Body

When we become aware that we may have to give a speech, we begin a process within ourselves that can be quite complex. By understanding how our psychological and physiological systems work together to help or hinder our process, we'll find ourselves better able to control our own public speaking experience. While these systems operate almost identically for everybody, it is the perception of these experiences that may differ dramatically from person to person. Milton and Annette offer interesting perceptions on the prospect of giving a public speech. Milton describes his public speaking experience as follows:

One of the worst classes in my academic experience was my freshman public speaking class. I tried everything I could think of to get out of having to take the class, but for somebody interested in the business field, it was a requirement. I've seen a lot of good speakers out there. People who could stand up in front of fifty or five hundred people and talk as if they were talking to their best friends. I also knew that I wasn't one of these people. I think I started getting nervous about my first speech around the day I bought the textbook for the class! I mean, my heart started racing, my mouth got dry, and my hands started sweating right there in the bookstore! Martin Luther King, Jr. I'm not, and I just knew I would make a fool out of myself.

Annette described the same experience a different way:

When I found out during the interview that my job would require my making informative presentations to outside interest groups, I knew this was the job for me. I remember the second interview for my current position, when we started talking about these speeches. I've always loved being on "center stage" and this seemed like just the thing. I recall I started getting excited right then, in the interview. I could hardly sit still, because I knew that this was the element of my new job that would make me successful. In fact, just thinking about that interview makes me remember the adrenaline rush I got when I imagined myself standing in front of these people, all their eyes turned to me, and me with their full attention.

Wow! Who is this Annette person anyway? Do people really feel like that about public speaking? Is she for real? Well, yes. There are some people that go out of their way to find situations that will allow them to give public speeches. Not many, but a few. What's really interesting is to notice that Milton and Annette both describe the *same physical responses* to the same situation. However, one gets the sense that Milton wanted to go running out of the bookstore, whereas Annette wanted to go running up to the lectern. What differentiates Annette's excitement from Milton's terror?

Our body is designed to react to strange or threatening situations in such a way as to allow a large range of options and possible responses. Long ago, it was important for us as humans to develop an instinct that would protect us from danger. This instinct in the face of physical threat, commonly called the **fight or flight response,** became a characteristic of early humans that aided the species in overcoming many evolutionary challenges. If Jane and Joe Cavepeople had not learned that certain creatures (the occasional woolly mammoth or, perhaps, other cavepeople) posed a threat to their existence, and had they not developed an instinctive ability to detect and react to this threat, then, as one scholar has put it, we would all be descended from a long line of extinct ancestors!

The problem with this fight or flight response is that we have not only learned it well; we have learned it *too* well. Certainly, we still face physical dangers in everyday life. Walking across the street and realizing that a car is speeding in our direction may require an immediate, instinctive response. Hopefully, in this case we will choose the flight option, since fighting an oncoming vehicle may not lead to a desired outcome. There are other times when our level of stress may be so great—such as when we think about standing in front of a group of people and delivering a speech—that we essentially mislead our body into thinking that we are in physical danger, that the fight or flight response is appropriate, when actually it is not.

Except for some notable exceptions, it is rare that a public speaking situation will put you at physical risk. It is even more unlikely that your audience is actually going to charge the podium when you make your presentation. You know that, your audience knows that, and you know that your audience knows that. Even so, if your level of anxiety about giving a speech is high, you may still experience many of the effects of the fight or flight response when you face your audience.

Physiological Reactions

When an individual faces a stressful situation, such as public speaking, the body passes along the stress signal to the hypothalamus and thalamus in the brain. When the hypothalamus receives this signal, it in turn activates two of our body's fight or flight systems: the autonomic nervous system and the endocrine system.

The autonomic nervous system then activates several other subsystems in our body. Involuntary body functions such as heart rate, breathing, and blood pressure are affected. Usual results are increased heart rate, higher blood pressure, and increased rate and depth of breathing. Further, the pituitary gland orders the release of aldosterone, which increases blood pressure; cortisol, which increases blood sugar and energy; epinephrine (adrenaline), which increases energy; and several other stimulating chemicals into the body. As a result, we may experience anxiety, flushing of the skin, tremors in our voices, a decrease in body temperature, dryness of the mouth, or a quivering in various extremities of our bodies. Not everybody has the exact same reaction, but most people will experience at least one or two of these symptoms when faced with a high stressor such as public speaking. The difference is in how the speaker *perceives* the public speaking situation and how the speaker *reacts* to the fight or flight response.

Behavioral Reactions

As mentioned before, the most common, and most problematic, behavioral reaction to the public speaking event is to simply attempt to avoid it. Total avoidance is common and can be achieved by simply not accepting the invitation or request to speak. However, social, job and peer pressures sometimes make this total avoidance unrealistic.

The next most common avoidance reaction is to make excuses and rationalizations. We attempt to do this through finding reasons for not giving the presentation. These reasons are as varied as the possible speaking situations, but can include such statements as "I'm not the right person for this speech," or "I really don't have time to do the research for a good presentation," or "You know, I'll try to get out of that dentist appointment on that day, but I'm not really sure that I can."

Given that we can't totally avoid the situation and that we can't excuse ourselves out of it, we are left with what is probably the most uncomfortable and likely avoidance reaction: procrastination. If the excuses we make with others do not succeed in relieving us of the responsibility for giving the speech, then the excuses we use with ourselves will at least put off the inevitable.

Unfortunately, procrastination creates a spiral that can be both self-defeating and self-fulfilling. It can be self-defeating in the sense that, by putting off the preparation for our presentation, we also keep ourselves from having the time necessary to do a good job. Putting together a speech requires preparation. There is some research that needs to be done, plus some forethought that needs to go into the presentation. As we begin the research or as we sit down to construct an outline, we soon realize that we are committing ourselves to something that we really feel uncomfortable doing. As a result, we wait as long as possible to do the necessary preparation and by so doing, we create our **self-fulfilling prophecy.** In other words, we have a sense of foreboding that says we aren't going to do a good job on this public speech. Then, through procrastination, we guarantee it. Without proper preparation and practice, even the best public speaker is destined to fail.

We have then proven the point we set out to state at the beginning: We can't give a public speech. At the least, we feel we have proven the point when we don't do as well as we could have. Of course, the real reason in this case is that we didn't prepare properly. It will serve as another uncomfortable situation which will make us avoid the next public speaking situation even more. Now not only do we feel as if we can't stand up in front of people to make a presentation, we have at least one experience we can recall where we *did* give a presentation, and we did a poor job of public speaking. In addition, somewhere deep down, we know that the reason we didn't do well is because we didn't work at it, which adds to our sense of failure: failure to others, failure to our audience, and failure to ourselves.

Psychological Symptoms

The feeling of failure associated with avoidance actually can, and frequently does, appear before you've even given your presentation. First, there is the "I'm going to fail" period where we may find ourselves being overachievers.

Mind and Body 13

What the audience sees   *What the speaker feels*

We may spend hours designing the "perfect" visual aid. Or we may make trip after trip to the library or other resource provider to find just one more piece of research or to read one more relevant argument, convincing ourselves the whole time that we are going to do a poor job or "look stupid."

Then, during the speech, there is the "I'm failing" period. Many of us find that we are hyper-aware of the physiological reactions to stress we are experiencing. We perceive that the slight leg shakiness we are feeling looks to the audience as if we are doing an Elvis impersonation. The red blotches we can see on our neck in a mirror appear to the audience as an atlas representation of the world's continents.

During the actual speech, many people also experience what is called **cognitive disruption.** This is a rather academic-sounding term for what most of us would call a difficulty in keeping concentration. As just mentioned, there's the hyper-focus on ourselves. We must also remember that the body has geared up in a way that gives us much excess energy. Our minds tend to wander, especially if we haven't prepared enough for the speech to begin with. We can find ourselves easily distracted or forgetting an idea in midthought.

Then, of course, there's the "I was a failure" period. We are our own worst critics. Invariably, we will feel that we have done a much less satisfactory job than most of our audience will feel we have done. Our perception of our performance is clouded by our own self-doubts. A speech that to the audience seemed perfectly fine, can, to us, seem like an abysmal failure. Unfortunately, we don't often weigh the evidence for or against our performance. Rather, we depend on our feelings about how well we've done. And since we've just completed something that was horrifying to us, it's not surprising that we might think we did a poor job, when actually we did just fine.

It is important to recognize our personal reactions to the public speaking situation for several reasons. First of all, it's a common misconception that "I'm the only one who experiences...." For those who tend to get red blotches on their face and neck, you should realize that many people experience red blotches. Those who tend to avoid the public speaking situation altogether should realize that avoidance is a common reaction to the fear-inducing stimulus of public speaking. Also, if you find that your thoughts are scattered when you attempt to give a speech, you need to know that many successful public speakers have learned to deal with the same distractions.

That's the bottom line. Many successful public speakers *have* learned to deal with their phobic feelings about speaking, a subject we will discuss in coming chapters. That's the good news. If your hands shake, your knees quiver, you get a dry mouth, or you feel dizzy when you get in front of an audience, take heart. These reactions are not necessarily reserved for bad public speakers. Good public speakers are usually considered good because they have learned methods by which they can control their fear. Unfortunately, we compare ourselves *before* we even give a speech to what we *think* a good or bad speaker looks like. And usually, we decide we look more like a bad speaker than a good one. This is due, in large part, to what we know about public speaking and to our preconceived beliefs and misconceptions.

Chapter Three
What We Know and What We *Think* We Know

When you imagine a good speaker, what do you see? What do you think constitutes a bad speaker? What other thoughts or ideas are waiting for the opportunity to jump out and sabotage your efforts as a public speaker?

The "Good" Speaker

Everybody who gives a public speech has some idea as to what makes a good public speaker. Unfortunately, for many of us, the idea of a good public speaker would, by another person's standards, be an outstanding public speaker. In other words, we sometimes set ourselves up to perform as a public speaker in a way that is practically impossible to achieve.

That is not to say that you can't be a good speaker. However, by setting your goals to unrealistic heights, you are inevitably going to disappoint yourself. Perhaps (and probably) not your audience, but your own expectations will be diminished. Most of us can look at Martin Luther King Jr., or Maya Angelou, or Lee Iaccoca, and say to ourselves, "I could never be a speaker like that." But then, the negative message in our brain becomes, "I could never be a speaker." If we begin to define a good speaker by the characteristics of a great speaker, then we will find it difficult to ever accept the fact that we might, ourselves, be good speakers.

The "Bad" Speaker

On the other hand, if we are not careful, and especially if we are not very confident about our skills, we may define a bad speaker as a speaker with our own characteristics. Actually, it is more likely that we define a bad speaker by the absence of the characteristics that we use to describe a good speaker. For example, we may say that a good speaker is one who speaks confidently. For one thing, we do not often define the speaker's characteristics in very definite terms. We usually say that we "know" a confident speaker when we see one. Therefore, a bad speaker is one who is *not* confident. How do we know? We depend on the same vague observations; that is, we can "tell" when the speaker is not confident.

Our definitions of good and bad speakers might include statements that *seem* to be specific when actually they are not. We might say that a good speaker maintains good eye contact. What do we mean by "maintains?" Does that mean a good speaker *always* looks at the audience? What do we mean by "good eye contact?" Does that mean that a speaker can maintain bad eye contact? If so, how?

What we probably mean is that a good speaker looks at the audience often and looks at various audience members or areas of the audience when speaking to them. But, in our mind, it is easy to use the vagueness of "good" and "maintains" in order to prove that we are *not* good speakers. By not thinking specifically about what makes good eye contact, it is simple for us to simply imagine that we are not capable of doing it.

That's the case with all of the characteristics we consider to be proof of a good speaker. If we are not entirely sure what we mean, the easiest avenue for us to take is the one that leads to, "I can't do it." If we're not careful, we will proceed to do everything in our power to prove that we are right, that we can't do it. This is the self-fulfilling prophecy mentioned earlier. Once we have decided that we will fail, it is only natural that our actions will reflect our thoughts: We will act as if we have already failed.

Part of the reason for this self-fulfilling prophecy is that we orient ourselves to regarding the speech as a performance, rather than as a communication event. In so doing, we enact probably the most common and most harmful of the misconceptions about public speaking—that the speech is a performance. By focusing on the performance of a speech, we focus on ourselves. If instead we were to turn our attention to what we are trying to *achieve* in the speech, then we would relieve a lot of personal pressure and increase our chances for an effective speech.

Performance Orientation = Evaluation Orientation

The performance approach to public speaking has been taught, and in some cases is still being taught, in many classrooms, seminars, and workshops. The philosophy of this approach is that a good speaker looks, sounds, and acts like a skilled orator. Back in the time of Aristotle, an entire rhetorical practice was based on teaching speakers to *appear* credible, honest, and trustworthy. This philosophy was, of course, not totally agreed upon by the great thinkers. Many of the philosophers of the time felt that it was a speaker's job to speak *with* the audience, not to enact some performance with grace and flourish. If the speaker were indeed able to perform well *and* persuade his audience, then all the better. But it was the communicative *intent* that was seen by some as more important, not the communicative performance.

We still have these different approaches today. The one that most of us tend to adopt is the **performance orientation.** From the time of our elementary school book reports and recitations, we have been trained that a speaker "performs" a speech for the audience. This orientation produces a lot of uncomfortable pressures surrounding the public speaking event.

For one thing, by adopting a performance orientation, we put ourselves in the spotlight of the event. A performance implies that there will be an audience watching us for the purpose of enjoying our display. We see ourselves more in the role of actor than of communicator and in so doing, focus on the audience as a third party who needs to be appeased. The actor, for example, knows whether or not he or she has been successful by the applause given from an audience, or the rapt attention focused on the performance. This audience response is a form of approval; it shows a positive evaluation of the player by the audience.

While public speakers enjoy applause, and audiences enjoy applauding good speakers, it is not the evaluation of performance that the speaker should be focused on. When we adopt a performance orientation to public speaking, we tend to think of the speech only in terms of how well we will do as an actor. We fantasize about moving gracefully across the stage, with smooth, sweeping gestures that emphasize and illustrate our points. We imagine our voice, strong and confident, sounding a fluent and compelling set of words so that the audience is impressed with both our presence and our delivery.

The fact of the matter is, if we were to ask the audience members after the speech whether or not the speech was successful, most of them would base their answer on one thing and one thing only. Did they understand what the speaker was trying to accomplish? Did they find the speech to be informative? Were they persuaded by the evidence and analogies used by the speaker? In other words, did the speaker achieve the intended purpose behind the speech?

Because we tend to focus on performance, we also tend to focus on the evaluation of ourselves by the audience. The good actor is applauded, with shouts of *bravo* and congratulations after the performance. The bad actor is booed off the stage and finds that he or she gets little or no support after the performance. Nobody wants the type of negative evaluation that an audience gives to a poor comedian or actor. The pressure of a performance evaluation is intense. Yet it is that sort of pressure we normally exert on ourselves.

By now you are probably thinking, "Fine. If it's not a performance, then what exactly *is* a public speech?" A public speech is an opportunity for a speaker to communicate an idea or ideas to a group of people. It is an opportunity to inform or persuade an audience in accordance with the proposed purpose of the speech and the intent of the speaker. That is it. That is all. A speech defined in that manner is successful under one condition; that the speaker communicates effectively with the audience. Not *to* the audience. We communicate *to* an audience when we perform for their observation. A successful speaker involves the audience through compelling content. In fact, we focus 95 percent of our energy on having a good delivery style. Yet delivery is only important inasmuch as it adds to or takes away from the purpose of the speech.

If you allow yourself to think of public speaking as a conversation, rather than as a performance, you will find that you have relieved a great deal of pressure that goes along with being an actor. A good speaker may occasionally stutter, or perhaps have a voice that is a little softer than might be desired. But if that speaker has information that the audience needs to have, or has an opinion that the audience recognizes as compelling enough to consider, then the stuttering, soft-voiced speaker is a more effective public speaker than the slick, smooth, fluent speaker who really has nothing to say.

In fact, audiences are a lot more forgiving than we usually give them credit for being. Think about the last time you were in an audience for a public speech. If the speaker stutters, or has a unique dialect, or perhaps looks more at the podium than at the audience, we do indeed notice it. Briefly. Then, we usually ignore it and focus our attention on *what the speaker is saying*. We say to ourselves, "Oh, she's nervous" or "What an interesting dialect." Then we forget it. Because if we are there to hear a speaker, our purpose as audience members is to receive information. We watch a comedian to be entertained, but we listen to a public speaker to be informed.

Let's imagine for a moment that you buy into the idea that the public speaking event should be seen as a conversation rather than as a performance. We will discuss later some specific ways you can change your approach to speech making so that you can recognize and achieve the communication goal more readily than the performance goal. Are you still nervous? Probably. Why? Probably because there are still many elements of the public speaking situation that you are unsure about. In fact, this "fear of the unexpected" can be the primary cause for your speech anxiety.

Fear of the Unexpected

Another element of the fight or flight response that is important to remember is that this instinctive survival response was designed to be *reactive*. In other words, we developed this instinctive response to physical danger that can occur in a moment's notice to danger that is *unexpected*. It might even be that we know a danger is going to exist, but we are not sure how well we will fare when facing this danger. Again, it is the unexpected or unpredictable outcome that makes us the most nervous. Therefore, one of the ways to deal with our anxiety about making a public speech is to make the speaking event as predictable as possible

What really *is* going to happen when you give your speech? Is the audience going to rise up in exultant ovation? Are they going to mob the stage when you're finished, attempting to get an autograph or a lock of hair? Are you going to have to get an unlisted number because of all the calls you receive at home to praise you for your outstanding presentation?

What makes us the most nervous is fear of the unexpected.

Or will your audience literally "boo" you off the stage? Will they be so bored that your speech is constantly disrupted by the sound of bodies falling asleep and sliding out of chairs? Will they bring fruits and vegetables to fling on stage during your speech? Or will the host of the event stand up at about the midpoint of your presentation and ask you to please sit down and shut up?

Well, no. None of these things is actually likely to happen. Neither will you be the greatest speaker that the audience has ever heard, nor will you be the worst. It is unlikely that you are going to put your audience into a state of awe because of your brilliant oratory style and it is unlikely that you will be chased from the building because of your horrible speech. What is most likely is that your presentation will fall squarely in between these extremes. There will be some elements of your speech that you will have done very well. There will be other aspects that could be improved upon. But that's the case with all of our endeavors. It's the rare situation that can't be improved, and it's the rare situation that is the best possible scenario.

The point here is that you must consider the public speaking situation realistically. Think about the likely responses and questions your audience may have when you've completed your speech. Then focus on those responses and questions. This will serve the purpose of taking your attention away from your delivery as well as allowing you to prepare a speech that is ready for the most likely questions or reactions.

You should strive to make the public speaking event as predictable as possible. You should not consider your speech to be a performance, but rather an opportunity to gain a response from your audience that will be beneficial to you and them. Consider the *realistic* outcomes of your presentation. It is unlikely that your audience will react in any extreme way to your speech, but rather will be supportive and want to see you succeed. Through practice, preparation, and planning, you will be able to overcome much of the anxiety you face well before actually giving your speech.

We've now covered the areas of the public speaking experience that lead up to your decision to be excited or anxious about the public speaking event. Through recognizing that speech anxiety is a common phenomenon, experienced by most speakers to some degree, you should understand that you are not alone in your feelings of nervousness and that this nervousness can be channeled into the excitement necessary for you to produce a good, solid speech. To make that energy a positive force, you need to develop some strategies for dealing with the anxiety that you know you're going to experience. The next chapter will give you some suggestions and methods to consider for changing anxiety to excitement and creating a successful public speaking event.

Chapter Four
Nervous Excitement versus Nervous Anxiety

When I have to give a presentation, I can feel the adrenaline all the way to the ends of my hairs. I start fluttering my fingers and I can't stand still. When I stand at the podium, if I'm not careful, I raise the heels of my feet up and down. Then, when it's over, I continue to be hyper. I swear, I could run the New York Marathon when I'm giving a speech.

—ANGELO, 22

While it may be difficult for Angelo's audience to listen to his presentation while running through Manhattan, he probably does have the energy to "run the New York Marathon" when he's giving a speech. Earlier, we discussed all the systems the body fires up when we're faced with a stressor. We also discussed the fact that those physiological systems engage regardless of whether the stressor is a threat or not. When faced with the unknown, the body typically plays it safe and acts as if what you are facing is a threat. In fact, it's your brain that's actually telling your body to shift into high gear. So it's your brain, the way that you *think* about the public speaking situation, that has to be addressed first.

Interestingly enough, if Angelo were to do some mild form of physical exercise before he gave his speech, he would be engaging in the easiest method to control the nervous feelings he experiences during the presentation.

A brisk walk around the building or a couple of push-ups in the office (honestly!) can help relieve some of the stress because it "fools" the body into using up some of that extra fuel. Remember, the body is gearing itself up for physical reactions. If you undertake some sort of light exercise, your body will rapidly dissipate much of the chemical buildup that occurs when the fight or flight system kicks into action.

But, what does exercise, a physiological activity, have to do with attacking the problem psychologically? For one thing, while you're exercising you will probably think of other things besides your speech. That alone is worth something. More importantly, as you exercise lightly, the increase in blood pressure is reduced, the chemicals such as adrenaline are dissipated in your body, and the effect of these chemicals on the brain (and the effect of the chemicals on your body which then affect the brain) are rapidly reduced as well. In other words, exercise helps reduce the physiological effect on the psychological process.

Obviously, it's going to be difficult to tote the stationary bicycle with you to every presentation you make. But you can take a short walk, run in place for a couple of moments, or simply jump up and down a few times. Just remember that you're not really engaging in this exercise to tone up flabby muscles or lose a few extra pounds. The point is to just get the blood circulating a bit; so take it easy. If you get to the point where you're panting for breath, or your clothes are beginning to stick to your body, you're doing too much!

Relaxation

For some people, and in some circumstances, physical exercise before a speech simply isn't an option. While it is possible to find ways to relieve extra energy through physical exertion (one student of mine used to run her wheelchair up and down the hall a couple of times before giving a speech!), it is still not always plausible. For example, we may have spent a lot of time on our physical appearance and do not want to engage in any exercise at all. When's the last time you did jumping jacks wearing heels or a three-piece suit?

The alternative to exercise is relaxation practice. In fact, the two can be done together, and are quite effective in tandem. If you can't exercise, you may find that relaxation practice can be just as efficient by itself. And, while there are some relaxation exercises that require a lot of time and a lot of room, you can usually develop the skill to relax with just a few moments and with no special space requirements.

In his wonderfully thorough book, *The Relaxation Response,* Herbert Benson proposes that there is an equal and opposite reaction to stress that an individual can develop to help control the effects of the fight or flight response. Although Dr. Benson's book is about dealing with fatigue, anxiety, and stress in general, many of his guidelines can be used to help you control the specific anxiety felt when faced with a public speaking situation.

As stated earlier, the fight or flight response activates the sympathetic part of the autonomic nervous system, resulting in bodily activity that contributes to the feeling of anxiety and lack of control. The relaxation response, on the other hand, activates the parasympathetic part of the autonomic nervous system, resulting in such effects as slowed heart rate, increased salivation and digestion, and lowered blood pressure. In other words, the *para*sympathetic system is designed to offset the effects of the sympathetic system, the part that is causing you the most problem with speech anxiety. There are literally hundreds of relaxation methods that have been proven effective for some people at some time, including meditation, self-hypnosis, visualization, and so on. We are going to examine two methods of achieving this response. Hopefully, you will find one or both of these methods to be effective for you. If you already have a favorite method, or discover one that works better for you, that's great. Use it. You may even find that you're able to develop your own method of inducing the relaxation response. For most individuals, the most effective technique is the one that is a matter of personal preference, that is, the one with which the individual is most comfortable. With some experimentation, you'll discover a method that works for you.

With whatever method that is chosen, some people find it easier to begin practicing their relaxation exercise with the help of an audiotape. You may discover that, as your body relaxes, your mind tends to relax as well, sometimes making it difficult to concentrate on remembering what you are supposed to do next. There are many of these tapes on the market. There may even be a relaxation tape included as part of this book. If not, or if somebody has already taken the tape, you'll find an order form for a relaxation tape in the back of this book. If you do not already have a favorite relaxation method, you should consider giving the tape a try.

Whether or not you have a tape or a favorite method of relaxing, it might be helpful to briefly discuss a couple of different relaxation methods. Active Relaxation and Visualization are two of the most popular of these methods.

Active Relaxation

Although it at first sounds like a contradiction in terms, Active Relaxation can be an effective method of relaxing before a speech or anytime you feel tense. The principle at work behind Active Relaxation is one of "opposite and equal reaction." Simply put, when you take an already tense muscle, contract it even further, and then relax the muscle, the muscle will return to a state more relaxed than when it started.

You can test this method right now while reading this book. Take a moment to become aware of your right upper arm. Use your left upper arm if you would prefer. For that matter, this can be done to any muscle group, but we'll say the right upper arm just for the sake of conversation.

Notice the tension that exists right now in your biceps. If you're holding the book with your right hand, you'll notice there are some muscles that are tensed in order to keep the book upright. Unless you are a very relaxed person, and you haven't even gotten up from bed yet, your muscle probably has some tension whether or not you are holding the book with your right hand.

Once you think you have a fair idea of how your biceps feels right now, start to tense the muscle through contraction. Tense it as tight as you can without going into a muscle cramp. If you're still holding the book with your right hand, you're probably finding that it's getting hard to read because your arm is shaking! Change hands or put the book down.

Hold the tension for a count of ten. Now, relax the muscle as totally and completely as you can. Lay your forearm on your leg or on the table so you don't have to use your biceps to keep your arm elevated. Notice the tension in your biceps now. Most people will discover that the muscle is less tense now than when they started. If you can't tell a difference (or even if you can), do the exercise one more time. If you limit yourself to no more than about three times doing the exercise, you should find that each time brings about more relaxation in the muscle.

Now, imagine this exercise for your entire body. You need to stretch out on a bed or the floor, or at least sit in a comfortable chair. Starting with your

Active exercise is not always practical just before a speech.

forehead, work your way down your body, one muscle group at a time, tensing and then relaxing. The first time you do this, it may take as much as twenty minutes to make it all the way through the body. With practice and experience, you'll be able to move a bit faster.

While this is an effective way to relax, there are a couple of problem areas for most people. For one thing, it's easy for us to tense and relax our biceps. It's something we do all the time and we don't look particularly weird when we do it. But tensing up our face is another matter. To tense the muscles in your face you have to furrow your eyebrows, squinch up your nose, pout your lips, and wrinkle your chin. Except for one case mentioned a couple of years ago in one of the supermarket tabloids, nobody I'm aware of has ever had their face freeze in that position. But there is something encoded in our brain that makes screwing up our face like that almost laughable even if we're by ourselves with no chance of being seen by somebody else. So, if you have trouble with this part, first make sure you *are* someplace where you are unlikely to be seen. Second, if it strikes you as funny, then laugh. Nothing can be as relaxing as a good laugh anyway.

Another problem that can occur lies in trying to tense the muscles too much. You should tense the muscle *as much as is comfortable* to hold for ten seconds. If the muscle starts to cramp at all, you are tensing too hard. This may simply mean that you should try again without contracting the muscle group quite so much. Or, you may want to go on to a different method of relaxation.

A similar problem is that there are some individuals who may have physical challenges that make Active Relaxation inappropriate. If that's the case, remember that there are lots of different methods of relaxation. So find one that fits your specific situation.

The final concern with Active Relaxation is that, even if you become an expert, you are almost always going to have to find an area where you can be undisturbed for at least ten minutes. This can be a problem if you're at the local Holiday Inn and preparing to give an after-dinner speech to some civic organization or if you're at a business meeting and are given an hour's notice before having to speak.

Because situations are unpredictable, and because part of your goal as a speaker is to make the context of your presentation as predictable as possible, it is important for you to learn more than one relaxation technique if you can. Visualization is an alternative technique that, with practice, requires very little time and little or no isolation. It is also effective for people with physical restrictions when Active Relaxation is inappropriate.

Visualization

A lot has been said and written about Visualization in the last few years. In every arena from education to business, authors have touted Visualization as the solution to slow learning, self-defeating practices, and business failure, just to name a few. As a result, the term "Visualization" has come to represent several different concepts and approaches to taking control of your mind.

Like Active Relaxation, your initial attempts at Visualization Relaxation will require a quiet area where you are unlikely to be disturbed for a short period of time. Initially, twenty minutes should be adequate. Many people have discovered that as they gain experience with this technique, they need no more than two to three minutes to achieve relaxation, which of course makes this technique applicable in more public speaking situations.

If this is the first time you've ever attempted a Visualization exercise, take a moment to go look at yourself in a mirror. Full-length is preferred. Notice what you're wearing, the color of your clothes, the style of your hair. Turn sideways and get a look at your profile. Turn your back to the mirror and look over your shoulder. In other words, take a moment to see what you look like. This is an interesting exercise in itself, since most of us see ourselves a lot less than other people see us!

Now, lie down on the floor or in bed or sit in a comfortable chair. By the way, you're going to have to read through this whole section before you do this exercise because the next direction calls for closing your eyes. Your first goal is to visualize what you probably look like right now, in your chair or on your bed, from about six feet away. Play with this image a little. Imagine what you look like from just a foot or so away. Then imagine pulling back to twelve or fifteen feet. The imagery in your head should be like watching a video that somebody made while you were resting, zooming in close, then zooming back.

Now, for the sake of discussion, let's say that you are in your bedroom lying on your bed. If you're actually sitting in an easy chair, that's fine too. Just change the appropriate visual images as you read through this. Feel the sensation of your body on the bed. Notice the feel of the sheet or blanket on which you are lying. Notice the pillow under your head and the feel of your heels on the mattress. Try to become as familiar as possible with the things you touch.

Now, visualizing yourself from a few feet away again, slowly watch as the bed turns into a large, white, cotton cloud. Initially, you should do this very slowly, with the bed gradually fading into the round, soft shape of a summer cloud. With practice, you'll find that you go to this part almost immediately. But for now, enjoy playing with the image again. Start at the top and work your way to the foot of the bed, changing the mattress into a fluffy cloud foot by foot.

Once you can imagine what you would look like lying on a cloud rather than a mattress (or sitting in a chair), try to imagine what lying on a cloud would feel like. It would probably feel something like being suspended in air. Perhaps your cloud is warm. You may want it to be cool. Regardless, it is soft and very comfortable. Imagine how your head would feel on a cloud like this, and your body. Imagine now your heels resting on a cloud rather than some hard surface.

Once you've achieved this image, enjoy it. Nothing should happen rapidly for a few moments. As opposed to what many will tell you, you should not try to force your mind to be void of any other thoughts. Lots of thoughts will come to you. Let them. But slow them down. Imagine that your thoughts are all trying to speak at once and you're making them hold up their little hands to take turns. Check your breathing. It should be slow and relaxed.

Now, before you come out of this comfortable situation, you should do a quick assessment of the feeling of relaxation that you are experiencing. Your goal in this assessment is to become familiar enough with how you're feeling so as to be able to recognize the feeling the next time you achieve it. Notice your slow breathing, the feeling of your relaxed muscles, the slow thought-processing you're doing. Notice how calm you can be.

When you're ready, imagine that your cloud is once again slowly changing into a bed (or chair or whatever). Don't be in a hurry, but as gradually as it changed into a cloud, the image in your brain should change into a bed. Imagine yourself lying on the bed again for a moment or two, and then open your eyes.

Neat, huh? Our mind is an amazing thing. We have an incredible ability to recall not only spoken messages, but visual, tactile, and olfactory messages as well. We can remember the exact sensations of how an object felt, or how something smelled. Visualization allows us to put this ability to work. You, of course, were never really lying on a cloud, nor have you ever. But you have felt soft sheets before, or the soft coolness of a breeze. When you try to imagine something you've never experienced, your brain will go through all the "sense memories" available to try to come up with what would be the closest sensation.

What you will have actually experienced is a type of self-hypnosis. Hypnosis is simply a *focusing* of the mind. You will have chosen to focus on something pleasant. But the real goal in this exercise lies in the final moments. Each time you do this, you want to try to reinforce the memory of your relaxed state as if you were in control of your thoughts and lying on that cloud.

While the brain is good at storing information about events that have actually happened, the mind will also store information about events that we have imagined. As a result, you will find that recalling that relaxed state becomes easier as you become more experienced at using this exercise. In fact, after just two or three times going through the entire scenario, you'll find that as soon as you close your eyes you imagine that you are lying on the cloud. Then, you'll find that you are able to simply "recall" the feeling of total relaxation and may not even need to imagine yourself doing anything at all. Believe it or not, with just a little practice you'll be able to recall the relaxed state without even closing your eyes. The trick is in being able to focus your mind, and like most of our other endeavors, practice makes it easier.

As with Active Relaxation, there are a couple of common problem areas you should think about. First of all, the most common problem with the Visualization exercise is that you may actually fall asleep. If you are going to use this technique to calm down before giving a speech, I also urge you *not* to use this technique to help you sleep at night in the beginning. Once you are able to bring about your relaxed state without going through the whole visualization process, then by all means if you need to relax yourself before going to sleep, do so. But don't train yourself to go to sleep during the Visualization protocol. The best bet in learning to do this is to try to make sure you are already rested (sleepwise) before attempting the exercise.

The second problem is that Visualization is **focused mind activity**. As a result, when you are focusing on the visualization, you are not going to be able to focus on much else. This is not an appropriate activity to do while driving, operating machinery, or doing anything else that requires your attention. Once you've learned to relax on demand, you may find that relaxing is anything but distracting. But initially, don't practice this exercise when you need to concentrate on anything else.

Some people find that their initial attempts at this exercise are difficult because they are having to remember "what comes next." This is a common problem that has a couple of solutions. You can record a tape or have someone record it for you. If you choose the second method, you should write a script that moves you slowly through the relaxation and visualization and then practice it several times before recording. There's nothing particularly compelling about the monotone of somebody reading a script, or stumbling over a particular phrase.

The second method is to purchase a tape with a visualization method professionally recorded on it. These tapes usually have a soothing background and have been edited so that the timing is correct and mistakes have been taken out. If possible, listen to the tape before you buy it. If you make sure the tape is published by a reputable publisher, or recorded by a well-known author, you are likely to be happier and more successful at your relaxation attempts.

Combinations

Many people find that they are able to combine relaxation approaches for an extremely effective personal relaxation method. For example, you might use Active Relaxation to achieve initial *physical* comfort and then Visualization Relaxation to calm your mind. Or you might use Visualization Relaxation to achieve calmness and then other Visualization methods to achieve further goals you may have.

As I mentioned earlier, the tape available with this book is designed specifically for the type of relaxation needed in public speaking, and is a "combination" tape itself. This tape is recorded by renowned communication scholar Dr. Larry Barker, and includes a method found helpful by many people, a sort of Progressive Visualization. If you find you have trouble imagining such things as fluffy clouds, you may find the technique included on the tape most effective. In this relaxation exercise, you will, through visualization, bring your body to total relaxation, piece by piece. Unlike the active relaxation mentioned earlier, you won't be tensing any muscles but will instead be relaxing them from the start. An interesting aspect of the tape is that one side has you doing the exercise from head to toe, the other side from toe to head. Research has indicated that some people have a personal tendency toward one direction or the other. If you find relaxing from head to toe isn't effective, go up the body instead!

Any combination that works for you is a good combination. You may even be able to Visualize yourself doing Active Relaxation. There are no wrong combinations. As long as you are able to find, and become familiar with, the relaxation response, you will be able to increase your ability to relax in stressful situations. And as this ability increases, you will find that preparing a speech becomes a much less nerve-wracking endeavor.

Controlled Substances

As a final word in this chapter, a couple of things should be said about using controlled substances. Many people attempt to "self-medicate" public speaking anxiety by having a few drinks before giving a speech or taking a sedative (or even smoking a joint). Without trying to sound too preachy, I have to say that this is a bad idea for several reasons.

First, the body's ability to overwhelm foreign substances should not be underestimated. For example, while alcohol has the ability to lower inhibitions and slow down the central nervous system, the body has an equal, and sometimes more powerful, ability to speed things up. So the tendency to overindulge becomes a real temptation. While one cocktail may calm some people after a particularly stressful day at work, it will probably take more than that to calm the type of anxiety many feel before they give a speech. As a result, the speaker will have two or three or more drinks before the speech. Then, rather than being calm, he or she is intoxicated. And, commonly, *more* worried about the speech than before. You may *think* you can't give a speech, but if you're drunk, you really do have something to worry about.

The other problem with using controlled substances is that our judgment inevitably becomes impaired. We imagine things are going better (or worse) when actually they are not. Our thought processes become scattered and it becomes even more difficult to concentrate than before. An impaired lack of mental ability is not exactly what we want to display when we give a public presentation.

The final thing to remember is that there is not a chemical depressant in existence that only calms the nerves. The more effective the substance is to calm us psychologically, the more likely it is to slow us down physically as well. This means that movements become overexaggerated because we attempt to compensate for the slowness. We lift our feet less high and as a result are more likely to stumble. Most noticeable is our tendency to slur consonants in our speech when we are under the influence of a depressant.

All of these physical symptoms of controlled-substance abuse can make the public speaking situation ten times worse than it would be otherwise. The main problem with using controlled substances is that the more you use, the less in control you are. And remember, our goal is to make an unpredictable situation predictable. This is an impossible achievement if we have made ourselves unpredictable by using some sort of drug to calm down. So as our past First Lady Nancy Reagan said, "Just Say No!"

Summary

Turning nervous anxiety into nervous excitement can be a challenge. But it can be done. Take the time to get to know your anxiety, how it feels, what the symptoms are, and when it starts. Then create a plan to deal with it. The cycle of nervous anxiety looks something like this: Mental anxiety leads to physical tension which leads to more mental anxiety which leads to more physical tension and on and on. You can break this cycle at any point: By calming your mind you'll calm your body. By calming your body, you will calm your mind. It takes practice, but probably not as much practice as you think. Making a concerted effort to get your brain and body under control can give amazing results in a short period of time. And when you see these results, you'll be better able to enjoy the excitement of giving a presentation rather than simply experiencing the anxiety of public speaking.

Of course, getting your initial fears out of the way is a big step in putting together a successful presentation, but it is only one step. Once you've begun to put into practice some of the exercises outlined in this chapter, you'll be better prepared to focus on the *important* part of giving a speech: constructing and practicing the presentation.

Chapter Five
Presenting the Speech

It is impossible to cover all of the possible topics that could apply to public speaking in the scope of this book. There are several good books out there that cover the subject of constructing a speech in more depth, and I recommend that you follow up this book by finding a few others that give you even more information. If you are reading this book as a part of a public speaking course, you will find many good ideas and instructions in your primary text. The only thing to really say in the scope of this book about the *writing* of your speech is: Don't forget the earlier discussion about procrastination. The only way you will feel comfortable giving a speech is if you are prepared far enough in advance to have plenty of time practicing and becoming familiar with what you have to say. Last-minute preparation is a nightmare for even the most confident and experienced speaker, so start putting your speech together early.

What we will concern ourselves with here is the actual delivery of the speech. Although you probably worry about delivery from the moment you know you are going to give a speech, the delivery of your speech is the final element of giving a presentation. While we sometimes get obsessed with how well we speak, the fact of the matter is that audiences pay less attention to a speaker's delivery than they do to the speaker's message. If a speaker is too quiet, or speaks too fast, audience members will typically acknowledge this to themselves, thinking "Wow, she speaks softly," and then proceed to listen to what the speaker has to say. In other words, as the speaker, *you* tend to think more about delivery than does your audience.

That is not to say that delivery isn't important. Delivery is important inasmuch as it adds to or takes away from the effectiveness of your speech. Delivery is an important element, but only *one* element in the public speaking situation. And there are several things you can do to make sure your delivery is as helpful to your goals as possible.

The first of these, and probably the most important, is in your decision about the types of notes you are going to use to give your speech. While many people successfully put speaker's notes together on $8^1/_2 \times 11$ inch paper, I recommend using simple index cards. They are cheap, easy to handle, and will help you avoid writing too much information to use in presenting your speech. Also, if your hand *does* shake a little, it is a lot harder for the observer to notice when you are holding notecards than when you are holding a full sheet of paper.

Note cards are developed from the outline of your speech by using the key words found in the main points, subordinate points, and supporting material. The note cards should contain only enough information to remind you of what you want to say and the order in which you should say it. Only in the case of complicated statistics or direct testimony requiring exact wording should you use word-for-word phrasing on your note cards.

Note cards are an excellent aid to remembering the content and structure of your speech while still allowing you the freedom to adapt to your audience on the spur of the moment. Here are some tips about using note cards:

1. Use *only* key words on your note cards, never complete sentences. If you write your speech out word for word on your cards, you will almost always be tempted to read it to your audience.
2. Limit the number of cards you use. The fewer you have, the freer you are to interact with your audience. One good rule of thumb is to use one card for your introduction, one card for each main point and one card for your conclusion.
3. Use 3 × 5 or 4 × 6 *cards,* not slips of paper. Paper is sloppy and unpredictable, whereas cards are easier to handle and look uniform.
4. *Always* number your cards. This tip can save you a great deal of embarrassment if you drop your cards on your way to give the speech.
5. Although typewritten is OK, there is no reason why you shouldn't handwrite your note cards, as long as you can read them. Cutting up your outline and pasting it onto note cards defeats the purpose of using notes and will make you sound as if you're reading your speech.
6. Remember that the note cards are for *you.* Use your own system of symbols, abbreviations, little drawings, whatever will help. As long as *you* know what they mean, they are acceptable.
7. The only way to successfully give a public presentation, and the only way to successfully use note cards, is to be prepared at least a day or so in advance and *practice, practice, practice.*

Why not write your speech out word-for-word, or memorize your speech? For one thing, the spoken word is noticeably different than the written word. When you make a complete manuscript of your speech, and then read it to the audience, it usually sounds exactly like somebody reading a manuscript. Boring! It is difficult to concentrate on your audience and your content when you are busy reading word for word from your paper. The normal reaction to a manuscripted speech is, "If you wanted me to read it, why didn't you just give me a copy?"

There are occasions where a manuscripted speech is appropriate, but these occasions are rare. If you are speaking on a matter that is of such importance that each word must be chosen accurately with no room for error, then a manuscript may be what you need. For example, the president of the United

States uses manuscripts when giving a speech because his words form policy. A company spokesperson may use a manuscript to issue a statement of policy because the spoken word could result in litigation. So it would be important for each word to be exactly spoken as written.

Most of your speeches will probably not fall into these categories, so a manuscripted speech is not the way to go for you. Reading a script is difficult, not only because it is hard to sound enthusiastic, but because it is easy for you to lose your place or stumble over specific words and phrases. The written word tends to have longer sentences and more difficult words to pronounce than the spoken word, so using a manuscript doesn't ease your burden, it increases it.

A memorized speech at least has the advantage of allowing more audience eye contact than a manuscripted speech. But for most people, a memorized speech sounds very much like a manuscripted speech. To actually memorize a speech word for word requires enormous effort. For an average, one page of text equals one minute of speech. That would be twenty pages you would need to memorize to give a twenty minute speech.

Memorization also increases anxiety dramatically. It is easy to see why: If you have memorized your speech, you will be more worried about remembering each word and sentence than about whether or not your audience understands your message. Memorization makes us concentrate on specific *words* rather than specific thoughts. This will also detract from an otherwise successful speech.

So the route you need to go, and that you need to practice, is speaking with the use of speaker's notes. By the way, this is called **extemporaneous** speaking, and is the preferred method for nervous speakers. Extemporaneous speeches allow the speaker to make eye contact with the audience and to sound more enthusiastic about the speech. These speeches are more like conversations. If you recall from earlier in the book, this is the exact perception you should have of your speech: a conversation with your audience. With practice, you will find speaking with notes to be the easiest method of giving a public speech. But it takes quite a bit of practice. Since you've prepared for your speech ahead of time, however, you now have the leisure of having the time you need to adequately prepare the delivery of your presentation.

The first step is to take the outline you drafted for your speech and use it as a script. Practice alone the first few times, stumbling your way through the speech until you are pretty familiar with the introduction, the progression of the content of your speech, and the conclusion. Then make the speaker's notes as outlined earlier.

Now, with your outline handy, attempt to give the speech using your speaker's notes. Be careful not to write too much on your note cards because the more you write, the more like a manuscripted speech your presentation becomes. And trust me. If the script is in front of you when you start to give your speech, you *will* read it. So practice a few times with just the note cards. If you get stuck, pick up the outline and get going again. Your goal is to get all

Chapter Five

Try to keep your notecards to a minimum.

the way through using just the note cards at first. Then, after a couple of times through the speech, you'll find that you are able to make your presentation while just referring to your notes occasionally in order to stay on track. By pulling yourself away from a total dependence on your notes, you'll be able to improve the other elements of your delivery, such as volume, rate, enthusiasm, and eye contact.

There are some simple rules about these other delivery elements that you should consider once you've practiced your speech a few times. Don't worry about these things initially; wait until you're somewhat familiar with your speech. Then you can start putting the icing on the cake!

Volume

In most cases, the nervous public speaker will speak softer than is desirable while giving a presentation. This reflects our lack of confidence in ourselves and essentially gives the impression that we don't really want to be heard. So speak louder than you think you should. To you it might sound as if you're practically yelling. But to your audience, the natural tendency to be softer will be offset by the attempt to be louder. The end result is usually a volume that is clear and understandable to the audience members. If you are one of the rare individuals who actually speak too loudly when you are nervous, or if you are faced with a sensitive microphone, then you should practice in front of a friend and get some feedback about your volume before you give your presentation.

Rate

Nervous speakers have a tendency to speak faster than they should when giving a presentation. There seems to be a hurry to getting the words out, perhaps because the faster you speak, the faster the presentation will be over. This is what I call "The horse smells the barn" phenomenon. If you've ever been a horse rider, you may have experienced the situation where the horse catches a glimpse of the stall while you are out riding. Many times, before you know it, you find yourself back in the stall where you started.

So the obvious solution to this problem is to speak slower than you think you should. As with the suggestion concerning volume, your natural tendency to speak rapidly will be offset by your attempt to speak slowly. As a result, your enunciation will be improved and your audience will be able to take the time to listen and absorb what you have to say.

Volume and rate are the two primary elements of vocal delivery that affect a speaker's ability to be understood. The combination of these elements affects your overall clarity as well. For example, if you are giving a speech and speak with a single volume and at a consistent rate, you are speaking in what is normally called a monotone. Varying the volume and rate of your speech is an effective way to avoid this problem and to keep your audience engaged in your speech. Think about a conversation with a friend. Sometimes you speak fast, sometimes slow. Sometimes you almost whisper and other times you almost yell. If you think of your speech as a conversation, it is likely that the variation in your speaking voice will improve.

Also, if you are concerned about an international or even regional accent to your voice, you should not become overly obsessed with clarity. Simply by speaking loudly and slowly, most of your audience members will be able to understand you quite well. It doesn't matter if you are from southeast Boston or Pakistan. The reason your audience can't understand you sometimes is because the words seem to flow together, and if you are soft-spoken the problem is exaggerated. If, on the other hand, you are from the Deep South, then you might want to pick up the pace a little. But not much. The problem is still that it is hard for the unfamiliar ear to tell when one word ends and the next begins. Speaking loudly and slowly will increase your ability to enunciate and your audience's ability to understand.

Eye Contact

Eye contact is another important element of public speaking. Although empirical research has yet to confirm the truth in this, we still believe that an honest person looks us in the eye. To build credibility, you should attempt to make eye contact as much and with as many people as possible. If you don't look at your audience, you can't know if they are understanding your message, or if they perhaps have questions they would like to ask.

There is also a kind of "dirty trick" that is related to eye contact. If we, as audience members, notice the speaker looking at us, then we feel overwhelmingly compelled to look at the speaker. It's a trick that school teachers have known for ages. So one way to keep your audience's attention is to make sure that you look at them. As a result, they will keep their eyes, and their minds, focused on what you have to say.

If you have trouble making eye contact with your audience, then begin by making eye contact with one member of your audience. Do *not* look over the heads of your audience. Unless you are speaking to several hundred people, the individuals listening to your speech will experience an urge to turn around to see what you are looking at. So make eye contact with one person. Then, as you become a little more comfortable, find somebody else to look at as well. Look back and forth occasionally from the one person to the other. If you do this fairly slowly you will actually appear to be making eye contact with several people. And, in fact, you probably will. You will also find that most eye contact elicits smiles or head nods or other positive feedback. As you receive this feedback, your confidence will become more steady and you will find that eye contact in general increases your comfort in giving a speech.

Movement and Gestures

There are only a couple of things necessary to say about movements and gestures. First, when you feel like moving, move. Second, when you feel like gesturing, gesture.

Actually, it's not quite that easy, but almost. You should attempt to step away from the lectern occasionally just to add some variation to your presentation. Sometimes the situation will keep you from doing this. For example, stepping away from the podium may mean that you are also stepping away from the microphone or out of the light or even off the platform!

Gestures in public speeches should be as natural as gestures in conversation. If you avoid sticking your hands in your pockets, or gripping the lectern as if you are under attack, you'll find that your natural tendency is to occasionally gesture with one or both hands. This is fine. In fact, it is perfect. We are used to seeing occasional gestures and, as you become more comfortable in speaking, your gestures will become more natural and relaxed. And, if you recall the discussion earlier about the stored energy your body has at that moment, you can see that gesturing is a way to help us let off a little of that energy.

One thing to remember is that gestures below the chest are rarely seen by your audience members. Try holding your elbows away from your body a couple of inches. By doing this you will actually raise most of your gestures to almost shoulder height or above. Your audience will then see the gesture and feel the emphasis that is implicated by some sort of hand or arm movement along with your speech.

Summary

Believe it or not, that's all there is to say about delivery. If you remember only one thing about delivery, remember that *you* are more concerned than the audience is. If you truly give your speeches from an audience-centered approach, that is, focusing on the audience when you speak, rather than on yourself, then it stands to reason that it is the audience's concerns that should be primary in your mind. If you will allow yourself to go with what feels natural, in most cases your volume will be adequate, your rate understandable, your eye contact plentiful and your gestures natural. Don't spend a lot of time worrying about how these elements of delivery *should* be. It doesn't really matter, as long as your audience can understand you without being too overly distracted.

Which brings me to a final word about practice. You really *must* practice your speech several times before making your presentation. And the last couple of times should be in front of a trusted friend. Try to have your friend sit in front of you at about the distance of the second or third row of audience members. If you find that making eye contact with your friend is distracting, and it may well be since he or she is the only audience member for your practice, then don't make eye contact. But do go through the motions of making eye contact with other imaginary audience members around the room.

And make sure your friend knows that you want honest feedback about your speech, not just about your delivery. Ask your friend if she or he understood what you really wanted to say, or were convinced about your opinion. Tell your friend ahead of time to pay attention to your main points and the flow from one idea to the next. In other words, give your friend some guidelines for critique. You can certainly remind your friend that you are nervous and would appreciate any criticism being given in a sensitive manner. But there is no substitute for getting the feedback of a trusted ally before you give your speech.

Chapter Six
The Final Word

The day of the speech has arrived. This time you spent a lot of constructive time in preparation for this speech. You prepared early and focused your speech at your audience. You've practiced your speech time and again and are armed with your index cards with key words and phrases, because you don't need to read a script word for word to your audience. You've gotten the feedback you needed from a friend and adjusted a point here and there to make the speech clear to the audience that you know so well. This is going to be a different experience than you're used to because this time you will have a successful public speaking experience. And all you need is one good experience upon which to build so that each successive speaking experience is more successful than the one before.

Now let's be realistic. Is your speech going to be perfect? Probably not. There will be points that could have been clearer, phrases that could have been enunciated better, and sections of the speech where your eye contact could have been improved upon. But that's the case with everybody, not just you. It is vitally important that you realize you are only human and are going to make mistakes. But these mistakes will be ten times more noticeable to you than to anybody else in the room.

So make your goals realistic. If you have not been able to make eye contact with anybody when you give a speech, then decide that this time you will make eye contact with three people, three times during your speech. If you have always spoken too quickly, then promise yourself that this time you will speak more slowly during the introduction and the conclusion. You have the tools now to prepare both mentally and technically for giving this presentation. You can do it.

To increase your odds even more, there are a few simple things you can do the day of the speech. First of all, go to bed early the night before. Get rest. Avoid alcohol and, if possible, caffeine. Both of these substances affect the nervous system, which certainly doesn't need any more agitation than it's getting already. Both substances are also diuretics, which is something *else* you don't need in the middle of your speech!

Get to the room where you are going to give your presentation early enough that you can walk around a little before people arrive. Sit in the audience for a moment and view the stage. Visualize yourself giving a good speech. For most people who are apprehensive about public speaking, the images we have of ourselves giving a speech are negative. We imagine that we forget the speech (you won't—you have notes) or that we will not make sense (you will—you prepared for this speech) or that we have completely missed the mark and our audience will hate the speech (they won't—you got feedback.)

This time, imagine yourself giving a speech that is interesting and engaging. If you are still sitting in an audience chair, imagine that you are actually an audience member at your own speech. And that you are *enjoying* it! Don't try to make the image in your mind of the greatest speaker of all time. Just imagine that you are an *improved* speaker. And above all else, *smile*! If you really want to trick your mind into believing that you're enjoying yourself, smiling will do it every time. It's hard to smile and be mad, and it's hard to smile and be overly nervous.

Speaking of being nervous, don't forget the discussion of nervous excitement versus nervous anxiety. Remember that it is good to be nervous before you give a speech. In fact, it is normal. Decide that the nervousness you feel is actually excitement and that you can and do have it under control.

If you have the opportunity, go somewhere quiet and relax a few moments before the speech. If you're going to be sitting at the head table or on the dais for a while before you actually speak, then get away from the crowd before you have to join the table. Just for a couple of minutes, breathe deeply and slowly and tell yourself that this is going to be a positive experience. Whatever nervous symptom you've experienced in the past will probably come back in some form, but it won't be nearly as distracting this time as it has been in the past.

Then, a few moments before you actually begin your presentation, try to recall the relaxation response that you've been working on. If it doesn't come to you immediately, don't panic. It's working, even you're not initially aware of it. One person I worked with in the past said that she could never get the relaxation response to kick in before she gave a speech. But she could *imagine* that it had kicked in, and therefore she was able to relax more!

While you are giving your speech, try as hard as possible to concentrate on what you're saying, not necessarily how you're saying it. This is why suggestions like "Imagine your audience naked" and the like are ridiculous for most people. For one thing, it is difficult to conjure up such an image (and you probably don't *want* to even if you can). More importantly, suggestions like that draw your attention away from the important element of public speaking—what you have to say. If you find that you are getting lost, then look more at your notes. But if you can, look at your audience. They are usually quite friendly people who are as supportive as they can be. Remember that the majority of people in the audience wouldn't volunteer to give a public speech either. They are almost always on your side.

When your speech is over, avoid the tendency to overcritique yourself. Remember, you expected to make a few mistakes. Recall them, note them, and decide that you will improve on those mistakes next time. More importantly,

look for the areas of your speech in which you did well. Did your audience understand what you had to say? Did they leave your speech at least considering your point of view? Did you give them knowledge they did not previously have? If you can answer yes to any of these questions, or at least guess that you successfully accomplished some of these goals, then your speech was a success. Give yourself your proper due. Pat yourself on the back for the improvements you made. And look for the next opportunity that arises for you to give a public speech. Each time will become easier and soon you'll discover that the anxiety that has made you miserable in the past can become energy that is exciting and enjoyable when you make a public presentation.